Debor

The Shadow Factory

Indigo Dreams Publishing

First Edition: The Shadow Factory
First published in Great Britain in 2019 by:
Indigo Dreams Publishing
24, Forest Houses
Cookworthy Moor
Halwill
Beaworthy
Devon
EX21 5UU

www.indigodreams.co.uk

ISBN 978-1-912876-20-4

British Library Cataloguing in Publication Data. A CIP record for this book can be obtained from the British Library.

Designed and typeset in Palatino Linotype by Indigo Dreams.
Cover photograph of Herons Green Bay ©Deborah Harvey
Printed and bound in Great Britain by 4edge Ltd.

Papers used by Indigo Dreams are recyclable products made from wood grown in sustainable forests following the guidance of the Forest Stewardship Council.

For Sandra, Catherine
and
my friend, Liz Kerr

'...the art is not one of forgetting but letting go. And when everything else is gone, you can be rich in loss.'

Rebecca Solnit

Acknowledgements

I am indebted to the editors of the following journals, e-journals and anthologies in which some of the poems in this collection first appeared: *Algebra of Owls, Diversifly* (Fairacre Press), *Domestic Cherry, Hailing Foxes* (Gert Macky Books), *Lyrically Justified Vol 3* (Urban Word Collective), *Places of Poetry, Project Boast* (Triarchy Press), *Riggwelter, The Blue Nib, The Dawntreader, The Robin Book* (Jane Russ, Graffeg Publishing), *Until the Stars Burn Out,* and *Words for the Wild.*

Other poems have been exhibited at St George's, Bristol; the University of Chichester; as part of the Live Canon installation at the Studios RCA, London; and at Ledbury Poetry Festival 2019.

Oystercatchers won the 2018 Plough Prize Short Poem Competition; *Mr Cowper's Hares* won the 2016 Hilly Cansdale Prize at the Wells Festival of Literature, and *The Albino Ferret* was shortlisted for the 2018 Wells Poetry Prize; *where he lay undiscovered* was highly commended in the 2018 International Welsh Poetry Competition; and *Holcombe Old Church* was commended in the 2019 Shepton Mallet Poetry Competition.

Thanks are also due to Colin Brown of The Leaping Word, Strange Cargo, and the Friday morning poetry group.

Also by Deborah Harvey:

Breadcrumbs (poetry), 2016
Map Reading For Beginners (poetry), 2014
Dart (fiction), 2013
Communion (poetry), 2011

CONTENTS

The Shadow Factory

The Good Dogs of Chernobyl

'Don't kill our Zhulka. She's a good dog.'

So they stayed where they were told,
they never lost their faith
not even when the buses left
and the fallen star hissed flame and cracked
the air was thick with ash, the rain burned black,
and no one told them what they were
no one stroked their crackling fur
or scratched their ears.

Now they come through underbrush
on paths of wormwood, cinder, dust,
their paw prints brand the bitter earth
and none of them will sit or stay,
these dogs that know no human touch
that do not answer to a name.

How to get poetry

Someone has just left a room
the armchair cushion is hollowed, warm
the book they were reading face down,
words spilling over the floor.

There's always a chair, a window
that might look out across a lake
or the pitch and fall of slate, a storm,
a stony ocean

so sit down, love, put down your things,
slip off your shoes
and let what sounds there are come
creeping in your ears

the conversations of clouds and birds,
the turning of worms, leaves, a key
in a hidden door.
Step through, look around you

let curiosity take you wandering
bridge any mysteries with what you know,
all those stories that were told
around the fire.

Touchstone

The place you need to reach
is not a leisurely stroll from the ice cream van,
it can't be seen through the windscreen of your car,
you have to pack water, compass, map,
leave behind every day that has passed
since you were last here
all those exhaustions, constrictions, slough them
like too-tight skins

And let your flesh feel the gravel of wind-thrown rain
the luxurious burn of summer gorse
and don't presume to be certain of the terrain,
arrangements of rock and light seem familiar
but everything alters in shifts of mist, see
the back of your hand is creased now and withered,
the skull of that horse stripped bare
save a few black strands of mane

And you too will be picked clean, isn't that
what you came for?
No demands, no expectations
only let your bones hold you up, keep your gaze
on the granite horizon
till all is lost
              and you are found
and the road back home is slow with cows
and quick with swallows

Glebe Lands

Once we've decamped here, unpacked our lives
from cardboard boxes, carrier bags
we'll start to overlay this street with *I'm-late-for-work*,
your bleary bus rides, walking the dog whose bark
might well annoy our neighbours.

To you all this will be new
a row of houses on the edge of a hill
on the edge of a southern city
with views to the Cotswold scarp. I'll show you
the shortcut through the lane you'll call a snicket

which long ago the women swept,
trimmed with ribbon for a motherless bride
lifting her hem on her walk to church,
whose only son's already grown
and left home in New Jersey.

But for now I'm holding my grandmother's hand,
she's wearing a hat hedgehogged with hatpins
a smile too wide to jump, and my cousin comes
running up the steps from making potions
behind the shed door that's labelled *Privut*.

It is New Year, I am six. On telly
children in covered wagons are dying of measles.
A man drowns in quicksand, his black hat left behind.
And we've hours to fill till my aunt gets back,
a dozen years before her halo stains the wall.

The Shadow Factory

Was it nightfall or the sun eloping with a cloud?
No one knew for sure but whatever the cause
the shadow factory vanished.

Workers peered vainly at rollsigns on buses
traipsed to the gates where they'd seen it last;
on encountering rubble and broken glass
shrugged their shoulders, sighed,
applied for redeployment.

Perhaps it retired to a sunlit meadow,
sat itself down by a puttering stream
far from the whine of lathes, the scream of Harrier jump jets

perfecting hand shapes from watching wild rabbits,
learning how bats navigate by sound shadow
on moonless nights.

Old Moulder's Almanac

♈ **Sun in Aries, full moon in Libra**

Now it's spring, does the panel advise direct sowing?

Coffins are not required by law
but it is an offence against public decency
to expose a dead body

♉ **Sun in Taurus, seasonal blue moon**

When the moon is blue, who will make it smile?

That bloody dog! Don't get me wrong, I like her,
it's just that every night she howls
at the earth

♊ **Sun in Gemini, the moon waxing gibberish**

Do the roots of trees eavesdrop on the dead?

Whispers rise in sap,
old wood attunes its Judas ears
taps dead man's fingers

♋ **Sun in Cancer, all the stars turn black**

Do terminal illnesses commit suicide?

Worm made flesh, dwelling in us
have mercy on us

♌ **Sun in Leo, Perseus takes a shower**

Who dare tell the pious they are dead?

On the south side of the choir
Bishop Beckynton and his skellington
squabble in bunkbeds

♍ **Sun in Virgo, the moon puts up its umbrella**

Who can hope to hold back the returnless tide?

She feels for her arms, her legs, her head,
the current strews her grist, she drifts
beneath the surface

♎ **Sun in Libra, trees cling to their gauds**

How to stitch fallen leaves into their bindings?

Infant truants from time will never learn to read
their unwritten pages

♏ **Sun in Scorpio, death tests its sting**

Who will dust the ornaments of death?

No horses or barn owls here, pale or otherwise
Nothing needs reaping with a scythe
Time's non-existent, we do not boil eggs

♐ **Sun in Sagittarius, night extends a claw**

Who can bear the dead wait of winter?

The stars are dark as snow against gauze skies
or the feathers of crows that perch on headstones
as required

♑ **Sun in Capricorn, the stars gobbled by a goat**

Whose fingers unravel rivers, re-knot tides?

Graves heave and pitch, corpses moan of feeling sick
while the stillborn slumber on, rocked in their cribs

♒ **Sun in Aquarius, thunder drops its fork**

Why are the sky's cracks filled with ruinous light?

In the bronchioles of trees sinister masses
The white-scrubbed moon presses a button,
retreats behind a cloud

♓ **Sun in Pisces, new moon in pieces**

On Ash Wednesday do dead lovers sift through cinders?

They've buried his ashes in the wrong place,
now she can't wipe the smile from her face
Her dust's gone dancing in imagined shafts of sun

Aconite

for IW

Were you called Iris for the rainbow goddess
or the stately flower?
Either way your name isn't apt.
There's nothing insubstantial about you
you don't drift through gardens in sapphire silks
and pinstriped scarves.

Instead you bundle about your business
with diffident squirrel glances,
earthed like the roots of the plant you brought in
to show us one Monday morning
exploring the lure of its petals, its deep-toothed leaves.
Wolfsbane tamed in your capable hands.

Though sometimes there were rainbows
in your classroom.
Refraction through jam jars of water,
a milk bottle chrysalis bursting with ice,
triangular prisms spilling from boxes
like ingots of light.

A Perfect Circle

They say that Michelangelo
drew a perfect circle for the Pope to prove his art.
Or was it Giotto or Leonardo?
The record seems unsure.

Later Sir Isaac Newton
no less a genius in his field
showed through calculus that even planets
don't orbit in circles

which brings me to my grandmother's apple pie
made without using weights and scales
more or less circular on its plate
bliss in our mouths.

Why set store by perfection anyway,
isn't the bubble of a gibbous moon
blown through the sky above Mardon Down
astounding enough

and that pair of buzzards over Salisbury chalk
their elliptical, spiralling double helix
won't you carry that memory in your DNA
for the rest of your life?

Mr Cowper's Hares

And so he sits without moving
holds them in his lap

not so tightly they'll take fright
leap through the window
scream up the lane
outstripping every attempt to catch them
hurling themselves from rock to moss to wild supposition
till they've gone beyond all returning
no longer know they have a home

and not so softly they'll take fright
bolt down the passage
out through the door
dodging the grasp of passers-by
plunging almost suicidal into tan pits
brought back half-drowned in a sack
caked with lime

and so he holds them without moving
pent between his hands

sees his reflection
in their mad amber eyes

Complicity

Her father had his favourites
tried to reserve the food put out for birds he liked
thrushes, blackbirds, blue tits, robins,
these were welcome

The dully coloured, cheapjack jesters
the ones like puddles under cars
he'd scare away with a rap of his knuckle on the window
while she watched, complicit
for having threaded monkey nuts on lengths of string
her finger red from pushing bodkins
through corrugated shells

                        Only something looking closely
sees a greenfinch deep in leaves, feathers mossed
with yellow edges, barred by shuttered sun

        Only something small and drab knows its beauty

Sensible Shoes

Years of pacing the wards have left you
as sensible as your flat-heeled lace-up shoes.

Not prone to entertain crises, dramas
you button their pyjamas, tuck them tightly into bed.

You rolled your eyes at Lacock Abbey when a ghost
walked through me.

As a student nurse, waiting for the last bus
you refused a lift from a persistent Fred and Rose.

Even this story you mention in passing
never tempted to dress it up, take it out to dine.

But all this was before our January tour
of mid Somerset churches

the final chancel carcase-cold, with some vast presence
malevolent, old, coopied inside.

Not stopping to buy a guide I fled to the porch
to meet you retreating with equal haste

your sensible shoes flapping over flagstones
and only cemetery snowdrops whiter than your face.

The Invisible Man

After six decades
and three continents of nothing to say, he says
Take me to see my sister.

So we meet in the pub, they clink ice and glass,
reminisce about thruppenny lots
from the chipper, their mother
hiding the Shippam's fish paste from their father.

Back at her house, in her dim front room
the door drifts open, No One slips in,
he has coat hanger shoulders, ties, plaid scarves
around his neck.
Beneath his coat he wears four suits, a navy blazer,
eighteen washed and ironed shirts.

His empty gloves clutch a carrier bag
it holds wingtip dance shoes, cash,
two one-way tickets to Perth,
the shopping list she wrote for her daughter
instead of a goodbye note

and now he follows us out to my car
slides in the back
buckles the seat belt
flicks stale cake crumbs from his sleeve

signs his name
in the mist on the window
his breath doesn't leave.

Tesserae

for BA

These squares of earth are landscape stripped to bone
singing in tones of ochre, sienna,
deep notes of burnt umber

the song archaeologists heard as they scraped
listening for pebbles, stone, crocks
brushing away centuries of sleep

till Fishbourne's seahorses started to stir
lumbering upwards, swimming
through air

over fields and orchards, gardens, allotments,
barrows and graves where what has been taken
is given back

to the song forgotten ancestors sang
rubbing ochre into the bones
of their sacred dead

back when the sea was ice-scoured plain
when the land we stand on now
knew nothing of names and edges

Seeing Red

for LF

He describes how he perceives a sunset

What people tell me is crimson
I see as charcoal grey
a shadow on the horizon

Crimson's possibly not quite right
I think and of course that's the point

His poems consider
patterns in snowflakes
fractals in cantilevered branches,
they sit at the window like Whistler's mother
understand the mechanics of stars
travel distances

                    mine can't begin to imagine
being distracted by sea green lichen
   emerald moss, a single
                        rusting
                              autumn
                  leaf

The Kingfisher's New Clothes

for CP

It turns out kingfishers aren't blue

those velvet hues we call turquoise and cyan
not pigment
             but scattered rays of light
that glance off the cambers of their wings
                                    in fact
their feathers are drabbish things
indeterminate shades remembered in legend
before they broke out of the Ark
swiped colour from sun and sky

Antediluvian bird
stitched from rough unravelling sack
I see you flit past dripping trees
perch and hunch before you track

your folded wings a coracle
carried on your back

The Future Tense

You sat in the second row from the front
small for eleven, plaits fastened with ribbon
plenty of room in your bottle green uniform to grow into
while I yawned with the gum chewers at the back
doodling Ziggy Stardust and hearts
in my exercise book.

By the end of September you'd disappeared,
your name pronounced with a Gallic accent
went unanswered at register.
You missed *Qui es tu? Où est le garçon?*
never learnt
Chantal cherche le chat dans le jardin

After Christmas you were back
your hair mink blonde, styled like an old lady's,
your skin was amber as if you'd been lying on a beach.
Only your teeth had grown and they
smiled and smiled
and smiled.

March came, your seat again
empty. We grasped
the past perfect, the future tense
and no one asked
Est-ce qu'elle est là, Katherine?
Où est elle?

The Fragrance of Clara Schumann

It's not that he's rude, not as such
but he can't get away quick enough once we're done.
There he flusters, the famous composer,
cursing his collar stud, watching it
drop through a crack between boards
while I'm still spread on the bed, laughing
sticky as the sweet jam tarts he likes
ooh he's a greedy one all right,
though they say he only gets it up
with girls who're beneath him.

Oh I'm not beneath him, not now
or all those other nights I ride him, sweating
to crescendo, his hands on my hips, his eyes
on honey dark horizons.

'Armed with madness for a long voyage'

After four paintings by Leonora Carrington

I   Self-Portrait: Inn of the Dawn Horse (1937-38)

It's lost its mane and tail
but she's set that old rocking horse rocking
so hard it is lifting, hovering in the air

as if it might follow its living self
the one that has leapt through the frame
and is cantering into freedom.

And yes, it's a dawning

Leonora, seated on a satin tongue
her demon hyena at her feet,
will soon be gone

as desire materialises beside her
casts a shadow, erases lines
that would confine her.

II Bird Superior: Portrait of Max Ernst (1939)

Far away
in a gilded country
where the forests are deep and dark
she paints maestro Max

all flounced out in feathers and fish tail,
his stinging stripy socks,
Leonora's shaman.

He paints her
tangled in briars and vines

she paints herself
frozen in the background
  watching him walking out of shot
    helpless to stop him.

Even before war is declared
she knows
   he's leaving

taking her light
trapped in his lantern,
the egg he will hide in the ice
of this barren lifeless mountain.

III The Artist Travelling Incognito (1949)

Why so paranoid?
asks the Spanish psychiatrist

She straightens the citadel on her head,
rearranges the extra eyes she's borrowed
from her cat's remaining lives

They're coming to get me, she explains,
In a submarine

Lord Candlestick with his strictures
Mother painting biscuit tins
punishing nuns, suitors, the spies of the Gestapo
entitled artists who would use me
as their muse

I'm sticking my necks out
my real head's the decoy
                    it will parrot
what you expect   I've kept
my umbrella in case it rains
                    I don't know why
I'm in disguise
                    none of them see me.

IV The Giantess (The Guardian of the Egg) (c1947-50)

No foam-born Venus blown ashore on a shell
She crawled straight from the mouth
of the whale

turned her back on the map of her journey
freed the geese that led her
to her unknown home.

As for the terror
that overwhelmed her
she's put it behind her

so let waves rise, mound themselves into hillocks
miniscule men fight monsters
saplings sputter flame.

She is brooding mysteries in her head,
her unhatched visions sprout strange
feathers in their egg.

Oystercatchers

'Aujourd'hui, maman est morte'
                    'L'étranger', Albert Camus

One day
the day she's been waiting for will come

and she'll take these words with her to the sea
unzip her coat, pull open her ribcage

let them fly as purposely
as oystercatchers

pulling the strings of the sky
and tide

lifting the weight from each blood cell
giving her permission

Blooded

After Pliny the Elder: Naturalis Historia 7:13

Then let's blind this tyranny of mirrors
blunt the edges of our bright pink plastic razors

Let's not be neat, compact, discreet
hide who we are in the palms of our hands or up our sleeves

We'll smear our foreheads, noses, cheeks
not with the blood of hunted creatures, stain of killing sprees

but with our blood, this ferrous musk
fecund, nurturing, the russet of red fox

Vixen-masked, in long soot gloves
we'll blaze our clamorous ways through scrub

burn ash paths through suburbs, towns
singe the edge of meadows, commons, forests, downs

scratching sparks from burnt-out stars
chasing flames that leap from heart to heart

Cursive

like gel pens
scrawling greetings
from an eerie otherworld

carousel horses
fairy steeds
they skitter and canter in circles
whirl
bare their teeth

Sweet-wrapped dragons
in midday glare

shrunk
to levitating bodkins
stitching cotton grass and sedge
                              the red
rosettes of hungry sundew
to brilliant sphagnum moss

until the evening sun
          streams slantwise
                    through prehistoric trees

               spotlights
          squadrons of damsels
          hovering over the water

contraptions of tissue and oxidised wire

their frail wings fingerprinted
by the falling dusk

Eleven o'clock in Leningrad

We wake to colourless sky
look at our watches, look at each other
wonder how many hours we've slept,
the best part of the evening, or round the clock
into tomorrow. Through our hotel window
the streets are empty, they offer no clue

Soon, as we exit the metro
this milk-light will deepen into dusk
there'll be red suns to the east and the west
the bridges will lift their arms over the Neva,
fail to reach either

                    Caught

in this blue night we're outside of time
in a city of shifting names
built on bones and water

Dawn Chorus in July

sleepless, on top of the covers
the window open

it's the singing that keeps you awake
these airless nights

more cobbled together than it was
but still stitched tight
to the point of puckering, enveloping,

heavy on your skin

hold it to the light
and the dawn pokes fingers
through its snagged and laddered weave

colours wisps of faded song
the brown of wrens, blue tits' cerulean

a blackbird's ruinous farewell

where he lay undiscovered

In the never-quite-dark
of those first summer nights
I heard police helicopters sweep overhead
seeking the heat of suspects in hiding
trespassers, burglars, car thieves, murderers,
cannabis farmers

It was blow flies that found me
After the buzzing, lascivious squirms
the memory of rotting plums forgotten in a fruit bowl,
then squadrons of beetles homing in
the family of foxes that fed on my lungs,
the bone of my shin

As for you lot driving past
after tiles for your bathroom, this week's fashion
upgrades for last year's mobile phone
who don't notice me in elders and brambles
on your daily commute to your home,
there's no need for guilt

You've not ignored insects crawling on windows
snowdrifted mail behind a glass door
and I like it here
Already a second year is turning,
I wait for dead leaves to tuck me in, ground frosts
soft as flannelette
               untongued, undone
I don't call out

Red Kites Over High Wycombe

I know they're here before I see them
my eyes on the road, the car in front
then snatching at sky for that russet
skirl, daubs of white underwing,
riffled pinions, twisting tails.
There must be eight – no
wait – a dozen overhead.

The first time I saw one swoop
as I stood at the window of your room
I thought it an omen.
Now I know they can't be owned, won't be
diminished to fit my need.
I'm a visitor here, shifting boxes and bags
from one drab impromptu lodging

to another,
and unfamiliar with this town,
the suburbs these natives survey
with ferocious intimacy.
When my job's done I'll travel back home
where red kites are rare and the air
trembles at their whistle.

My father is singing Rev Eli Jenkins' prayer over the phone

My father is singing Rev Eli Jenkins' prayer over the phone
He called out to my mother when I rang
and in the wait that is usually filled
by my saying something, or nothing at all
he started to sing

My father is singing Rev Eli Jenkins' prayer over the phone
Sometimes he forgets how to fasten his seat belt,
straps both arms tight to his sides
but he's remembered I'm visiting Laugharne
he remembers every word of this song

My father is singing Rev Eli Jenkins' prayer over the phone
and I wonder if this is his prayer too
and whether he wonders for how much longer
it will be answered
My father is ninety-five, each moment is numbered

My father is singing Rev Eli Jenkins' prayer over the phone
He's never cared for the Welsh, scorns their sentiment
has no patience with old grievance,
made an exception for my sake
for the love that proved my curse my mistake my

father is singing Rev Eli Jenkins' prayer over the phone
His voice was never resonant
now it's frayed and thin,
my father is singing me a rag
to wrap myself in

that winter

your life was cut too short
to shape a story

there's only your name, age
date of death

pegged in lead capitals
to your heavy concrete headstone

that winter
pianos were burnt as fuel

and your cradle
was ground too frozen

to dig up
parsnips, potatoes

Holding the Balance

Look to the west and north
rain is blurring the bones of the moor

smearing the outlines of hills and tors
as you name them

Here on Holne ridge
against ink-blotched cloud

sheep are wet as if freshly painted
and once you've left everything will be tilted

fleeces crest the river's rapids
stone will pour, crows dissolve against the sky

It's all right to stop now
not even granite stays unchanged

let the land hold its own balance
under this shifting light

Black Seeds

A wreath of sonnets

I

You're not yet two hours dead
but already there's more of you
in your worn misshapen shoes,
your dressing gown
slumped on the back of your chair,
your bald shaving brush
than is left in this yellowing waxen husk
I can't believe you were in there

Years before you died I saw your ghost
snagged in the branches
of my neighbour's apple tree,
the hair you still had then
was frosted lichen,
your skin cracked bark

II

Not so much as a bark or a whimper
You let me down, I'll tell the dog later
You could at least have howled once
though a phone call at two in the morning
can mean little else

It's so dark as I drive over
I check I've switched my headlights on
and my father's next to me, telling me

which lane I should be in,
which route will get me to my parents' house
before he's gone

The paramedics are here, my mother says
There's five of them, trying to get him back
but it's his time and I won't strike a deal with God

III

We strike a deal. If I drive to the shops to buy you Lucozade
you will drink it

It's all tilting backwards, you tell the nurse
as she checks your temperature and pulse,
the velocity of your leaving crackling in your lungs
as you tell fibs about your fluid intake,
scrabble for your medals in the tin by the bed

… this one's the Africa Star
the ribbon's yellow for the sand in the desert
the red is for the blood

When I was six I'd practise being dead
spread-eagled like a cowboy on the front room carpet,
toe over toe for my crucifixion
my head drooped decorously to one side

IV

His head has fallen to one side since the paramedics left
but I've read that dead bodies often move
and now the coroner's men are moving him from his house

Common law says
the only possessor of the dead body is the earth
but they're impounding my father's corpse,
his death at ninety-five they're calling *unexpected*
Maybe a policeman in his crowded bedroom
smelt bitter almond on his mouth

my father said he finished his mother off
gave her half the tincture in the phial from her doctor,
flushed the rest down the toilet
but his doctor's refusing to sign his certificate
now they will cut him open, I do not want him cut open

V

Only when a pear's cut open
can you know what you will get

crisp clear flesh or something dry and mealy,
rot only visible from within

It's not that those who idealise didn't know you,
just that they only saw your rosy ripening skin

and though it's true you mellowed as you grew older
you never lost that grit

or the wreath of black seeds that were lying
dormant at your core

I'll ignore (as you would too) the you must feels,
the assumptions of a wealth of happy memories

More reassuring are the messages that say *I know
it's complicated*

VI

The route I need to take isn't complicated
still somehow I miss the turning
as I drive up Beacon Lane
distracted by the red brick chimney
they demolished years ago
which was never the Brickworks anyhow
It's the only time I remember my father being wrong

Now he teeters on a kitchen chair
puts a flat battery in the clock
from the stock he keeps in the tea towel drawer

I saw some Cattybrook bricks in the dim-lit tunnel
running under the line to Severn Beach
traced the raised lettering with my finger
the old habit dying hard

VII

Your old habits died harder than you did
your final meal dredged in table salt
snakes and scorpions shaken every morning
from your slippers

     After you died
I found an empty snail shell,
white with brown spirals, nestled in my boot
I put it on the mantelpiece for safe-keeping,
when I looked it had crawled away

The clock by your bed stopped months in advance
at the minute allotted for you to die
Twice a day you tottered past it while it waited
with open hands

     A lifetime has passed
since the moment you died
with you not yet two hours dead

The Albino Ferret

After 'Salome' by Lucas Cranach the Elder, 1530

Frost fall, the wood ink-black
against a scumbled dusk

As I clamber down the muddy track
my dog sniffs, turns a watchful eye

By the warren a man waits in half shadow
clasping something in his arms and I've

seen this before, I know this unexpected whiteness
Malice in a harness, collar, chain

the murderous
beauty of a creature without feeling

and I remember Salome in her sumptuous hat
after the soft drop of her nets

after the sating of this naked
red-eyed hunger

Nature Notes

Kirsty, 23

stabbed in the neck and chest by her partner
watched by her daughter, four years old, who waves
from the window to a neighbour, the neighbour waves back

Joanna, 35

hears Will You Just Fucking Die as she lies dying
at the hand of her boyfriend, the one
she thought might be The One

Anne-Marie, 47

it's just a normal morning, she's always calling the police
though who'd have foreseen this, says the DI,
hindsight's a fantastic thing

                         the shame
of those who escape, but scathed
like hares chased so hard their blood runs to bubbles,
who can't survive, won't make old bones or whose bones are
old before their time
                         buckled from huddling in their forms
reliant on golds, the browns and tawns of too short stubble

and still as the man who stands above them
reaping the light

Holcombe Old Church

The snowdrops you planted under the tree
never took hold and spread the way you said they would.
Each year a bloom or two against moss
keeping their heads down, often missed altogether

frozen, it seems,
                    confined in the stringencies
your presence always demanded, that shrunk circumspection.

This first winter without you, in this lost place,
I imagine it's you shaping the landscape, your body
forming its grassy tumps
instead of farm buildings and buried cottages
long forgotten

                    and this massing of snowdrops
has pushed its shoots through your rib cage,
the shattered silk of your skin
to reach the spring.

Pairings

That April
back when I'd still make tea for two
though only one was needed

I'd sit at the table, watch the birds –
sparrows, wrens, the pair of robins
perched on the bird bath,

glad they'd made it through the winter,
that the male was courting his mate
with juicy wrigglers.

You're here now
but I'm distractible,
it's you who brews the tea

and as often as not
I let it grow cold
yet in the moment of its bringing

I'll open my beak, quiver my wings
as if we might still sing the quickening
song of springtime.

What the walls remember

I 1930s, patterned with pansies

I'm given the room that used to be hers
with its one-bar fire that doesn't work,
spider cracks above the window
from Anemone Bombing Raid,
flowerdy wallpaper
the same colour as Parma Violets

My red quilted dressing gown
hung on the hook
stuck to the back of the bedroom door
looms, an intruder shuffling in
My father redecorates in green,
paints the drawers and the tallboy white

The twin divans
with their candlewick bedspreads
stay exactly as they are
for me and the still dead Mrs Sweet
whose persistent not breathing
keeps me listening all night

II 1950s floral, blue on white (slightly damp to the touch)

Jesus is watching
from the chimney breast
as we kneel on our grandmother's eiderdown
and slide the glass across the wall,
both unsure which way around
we should hold it

We press our ears against the base
All I hear is the ticking clock,
its hands pea green in December gloom
which Jesu's lantern can't redeem
It's just the divorce, my cousin says
Uncle Ken's and Auntie Sally's

Don't be daft
I say, putting back the glass
Divorce only happened years ago
when Henry the Eighth was king
you know
like beheading

Centuries later
my cousin and I will both
take off our wedding rings
Reader, I cannot vouch for her
but when all's done I'll swear
I almost lost my head

III 1990s blown vinyl in red, gold and white

It peels straight off
Underneath, the thin plaster is spotted
with damp from a crack in the render
and the six-petalled flowers
embossed on the paper
have reproduced themselves

like mildewed ghosts of masons' marks
incised by compasses on jambs
of parish churches, vast tithe barns
and copied onto mantels, lintels, beams,
all the places witches, demons
might break in

Under sealant and fresh paint
let that which cannot be defined
the creeping mould, its curious spores
trap our nightmares in the walls
and when the light drains from the day
let it keep all dread away

Gottle o' Geer

In one dream you're
hunched on the recliner
I ferried from Cornwall
in the back of a friend's Morris Minor

the gift you hated without even trying
resisting the leg rest, the dual motor riser
falling asleep uncomfortably upright
your body askew

               a disjointed puppet
whose strings I could pull
now that you're dead
manoeuvre your arms into a hug
throw my voice, make it sound like you're saying
I love you –

Brown Dwarf Star

for CB

Marooned in your cupped hands
a juvenile starling

washed into our garden
on a tidal wave of fledglings
trying out their wings,
who mistook our patio door for air, crash-
landed on concrete

Stunned, eyes shut, she huddles
her feathers
chipped from layers of grey-brown slate,
a globulet of blood
crimson in the ebbing sun

What's the diminutive of little star?
starlingculus – starlingette –
or brown dwarf star
too small, too weak, too dazed to shine?

I stroke her back
with the back of my finger,
she opens her eyes, closes her beak
sits in the hollow of your hands

your gentle, capable, lifted hands

feeling the dusk beneath her pinions, her feet
gripping your palm till she's steady

ready to fly

Story

for DM

You've travelled further than most
from Lancashire gritstone,
Valleys coal,

stalwart pilot of your boat,
the Southern Ocean
swabbing the deck

In this next chapter
the waters are quieter, your habitat
towpath, hedgerow, chalk sown with flint

You investigate
landscapes in muddy puddles,
dinosaur bones in otter spraint

In the clamp of each winter
you hunker in lamplight
your narrowboat tethered tight to the bank

lodged like the paint brush in your hand
with you the colour
at its tip

Herons Green Bay

Sometimes perfection's too much
like on early autumn mornings, parked by the lake
in the space between daybreak and dawn,
when you know without counting there's seven swans,
four calling crows, one eponymous heron
feathered in gold.

Write instead this rain-smudged dusk
bent and rusted railings breaking
with you convinced you're plunging through them
and fifteen feet under you gasp and flounder
through ruined farmyards, orchards, mills,
fields of mangelwurzels sown for winter fodder

past the twice-drowned ghost of a village girl
dripping and squelching
upstairs to her bed
and not understanding that she's dead
as she glances at headlamps on the causeway
mistakes them for falling stars

Father and Daughter in Three Dreams

I

He is holding one of the ducklings
in one hand
his thumb and forefinger circle its neck
he tilts its beak
with the teat of the bottle
squeezes milk into its throat, she cries
don't do that Dad, they don't drink milk,
you might kill them

but he is certain
it will do them good
they will grow bigger, better, strong
and she begins to wonder
if she's wrong if
somehow she's mistaken.

II

They are moving
on opposite sides of the same wall
encased in diving suits, lead-soled boots, weighted
belts, those heavy riveted copper helmets.
Puffs of sand rise underfoot
from drowning carpets.

                    Communication
by gesture, lights or tugging on buddy lines
is not available to them,
the bubble streams rising to separate ceilings
go unseen.

She takes out a stethoscope
thinks she'll run it over wrinkled anaglypta,
remembers her helmet, that it's in the way,
the tips of the head-piece can't fit in her ears,
all she hears
                    is her breathing.

III

And there he is sitting beside her, sad and dead.
He is old, he is wearing his air force blue jumper
he is hundreds of miles away
she reaches to touch him, he's not as cold
as she thought he'd be.
                              She tries to tell him
he's in the wrong place, her fingers leave
imprints on his skin, he doesn't seem
to feel them.

                    Her other younger father
the one who still has teeth and hair
who's watched from his seat across the room
is starting to grin
                    She ushers
the helpless one outside
he is holding her hand like she's the parent
he's the child.

The Visible Horizon

Street lights have thrown
their grubby dust sheets over the sky

If I could only see the stars
I'd make my way to some dark hill
where they tumble
headlong to the ground,
tracing my journey by their braille
like a manx shearwater

or a dung beetle
toiling through the dirt

me and my dung ball
rolling along

Try yoga

'You know, I'm not at all sure
all this poetry's good for you.
I think you should try to empty your mind
declutter your bookshelves, try yoga, drink kefir,
I'll give you some culture.'

She takes a sip of her Earl Grey, it's made
just the way she likes
a smidgen of milk, a teaspoon of sugar
(slightly heaped)

and you can still see her at the window,
gazing up the grassy bank
past the cars in the car park to the gulls
feng shuied on the leisure centre roof

but the distance between you is growing greater
and she can't feel the roar that is passing
silently through mountains

as poetry's teeth close on your nape
and it drags you
unprotesting
deeper into jungle.

Heaney's Wake

All year
from winter to autumn
I see them most evenings

on high streets, down side-roads
slipping through hedges
under the bunting of parked cars,
charcoal running stitches
hemming the edge of dark. In April
vixens trail their kits
                    like knots
                              in hankies

Come September
                    flashes of amber – intermittent –
a youngster, trapped by headlights
                              panics on Southmead Road
                    spins in indecision,
          his currents short-circuiting, every nerve and instinct
                                        scrambled

After the wake
and the long drive back,
two miles from home and my bed
the shadows in my head give way to quick
anticipation

a dog-fox on Horfield Common
in Belisha beacon glare
waits on the pavement for me to brake
trots over the crossing with a twitch of his bristling
white-tipped tail

if I could
touch his fur, sparks would
jump and crackle

my spirits kindled by this sight,
this burning matchstick
to hold against the night

October

Somewhere I can hear a lark
a desultory bee out late in heather
mistaking the warmth of the sun for summer,
unaware the hour's about to slip
febrile mornings flare then gutter
darkness close over our heads.

Like bumble bees that cannot fly
oaks can't grow on this high ground
but no one's told them.
Piles Copse digs in on its steep slope
looping roots around heaped rocks
its leaves rust flags against a dusk that seeps
from cemeteries of peat.

If I could pour this honey light
store it in jars on cellar shelves
I'd dip my fingers in its gleam
until my skin grows green with moss
my tongue bleeds sap.

Notes

Page 9 **The Good Dogs of Chernobyl**: *'Don't kill our Zhulka. She's a good dog'* – Note pinned to the door of an evacuated house in the Exclusion Zone during the cull of pets and domesticated animals that followed the nuclear disaster of April 1986.

Chernobyl is the Ukrainian word for wormwood. In the Book of Revelations, Wormwood is a star that falls to earth and turns a third of the waters bitter.

Page 13 **The Shadow Factory**: Patchway Shadow Factory was built in 1937 to help meet the urgent need for more aircraft using technology transfer from the motor industry. It was demolished in 2009.

Page 19 **Mr Cowper's Hares**: William Cowper, the 18th century poet and hymn-writer, kept three orphaned hares as pets, and found respite from his depression in caring for them.

Page 21 **Sensible Shoes**: Between them, Fred and Rosemary West murdered at least thirteen women and girls in Gloucestershire and Herefordshire from 1967 to 1987.

Page 23 **Tesserae**: In 33,000 BC, the ceremonial burial of a body took place at Paviland Cave, now on the Gower coast but then up to seventy miles inland.

Fishbourne Roman Palace, near Chichester, dates from around 75AD and was excavated in 1960.

Page 25 **The Kingfisher's New Clothes**: The individual feathers comprising the kingfisher's plumage appear blue en masse and at a distance, due to the Tyndall effect.

Page 27 **The Fragrance of Clara Schumann**: '[Brahms] had an unpleasant way of … staring at [pretty women] as a greedy boy stares at jam tartlets.' Ethel Smyth, social reformer

Page 28 **'Armed with madness for a long voyage'**: The title is a paraphrase by Leonora Carrington of the inscription in Mary Butt's novel, 'Armed with Madness', which reads 'Armed with madness, I go on a long voyage'.

Page 33 **Blooded**: In Naturalis Historia, Pliny the Elder says that if a menstruating woman walks barefoot through fields at sunrise, with her hair dishevelled and her girdle loose, the crop will wither and dry up. Her glance will dim the brightness of mirrors and dull the edge of steel.

Page 35 **Eleven o'clock in Leningrad**: The original 18th century city of St Petersburg was built by slave labourers, at least 100,000 of whom died in the process.

Page 48 **Nature Notes**: This poem makes reference to the 2013 murders by their partners of Kirsty Humphrey, Joanna Hall and Anne-Marie Birch.

Page 49 **Holcombe Old Church**: The original site of the village of Holcombe in Somerset was abandoned during the Great Plague of 1665-66.

Page 51 **What the walls remember**: Daisy wheels or hexafoils are designs found in old buildings dating from the middle ages onward. It is believed that they served as ritual protection (apotropaic) markings.

Page 57 **Herons Green Bay**: Catherine Brown drowned in the mill race at Moreton, Somerset at the turn of the 20th century. The same fate befell the entire village fifty years later, when Chew Valley Lake was built to supply water to Bristol.

Page 60 **The Visible Horizon**: Celestial navigation is the use of angular measurements between celestial bodies and the visible horizon to locate one's position. It is believed to be used by nocturnally migrating birds, harbour seals and dung-beetles.

Page 61 **Try yoga**: The part of a tiger's roar that is too low-pitched for humans to hear can travel long distances and pass through buildings, thick forests and even mountain ranges.

Page 64 **October**: Dartmoor has three areas of high-altitude ancient oak woodland – Black-a-tor Copse, Piles Copse and Wistman's Wood – where conditions are so harsh, it's theoretically impossible for the trees to have grown there.

Indigo Dreams Publishing Ltd
24, Forest Houses
Cookworthy Moor
Halwill
Beaworthy
Devon
EX21 5UU
www.indigodreams.co.uk